Advanced Trading Strategies

Technical Analysis, Risk Management, and Pro Tools for Serious Crypto Traders

By Joe Correa

Published by Live Stronger Faster

First Edition

Table of Contents

Introduction

Welcome to *Book 8: Advanced Trading Strategies*, the eighth installment in the *Crypto Wealth Academy* series. If you've made it this far, you're not just a casual crypto enthusiast – you're on a serious journey to master the art of trading digital assets. This book is crafted specifically for individuals who want to elevate their crypto trading game, mitigate risk, and operate like a professional – whether you're trading from home or managing portfolios for others.

By now, you've likely familiarized yourself with the basics of Bitcoin, Ethereum, wallets, and the blockchain. You may have dabbled in buying and holding, maybe even participated in staking or DeFi protocols. But now you're ready to take the leap into advanced trading, where strategies are backed by technical indicators, risk models, and sophisticated decision-making tools. This is where casual investing turns into a data-driven profession.

Crypto is unlike any other market. It operates 24/7, is highly volatile, and is driven by sentiment, macroeconomic trends, and cutting-edge tech developments. Traditional financial tools don't always translate well here, but understanding the *foundations* of technical analysis, market cycles, and automated strategies can give you a massive edge.

This book will walk you through advanced concepts in technical and fundamental analysis, including how to read candlestick patterns, use Fibonacci retracement, apply moving averages, and master indicators like RSI, MACD, and Bollinger Bands. You'll also learn how to protect yourself with solid risk management strategies like stop-loss placement, position sizing, portfolio diversification, and trading psychology.

But we're not stopping at theory. We'll explore powerful trading platforms like TradingView, tools for automated trading like bots and APIs, and how to backtest your strategies before deploying capital. Whether you're swing trading, day trading, or arbitraging across exchanges, this book gives you a comprehensive roadmap to trading with confidence.

You'll also discover how to use sentiment analysis tools, monitor on-chain data, and recognize whale movements and manipulation patterns — all critical for success in today's fast-moving markets. And because crypto is global, we'll review regulatory differences and how they may impact your trading decisions depending on your jurisdiction.

This book is practical, real-world, and designed for implementation. Each strategy will be paired with examples, tool suggestions, and guidance on how to avoid common traps. You'll learn what works, what doesn't, and how to continually improve using feedback loops, journaling, and metrics.

Let's be clear — trading is not gambling. It's not about getting lucky or finding the next moonshot. It's about managing risk, reading the market, and executing high-probability strategies over time. If you're ready to approach crypto trading like a professional and start leveling up your results, this book will be your guide.

Let's get started.

Chapter 1: Core Principles of Successful Crypto Trading

Trading cryptocurrency successfully requires far more than luck or speculation. It demands a structured approach grounded in discipline, risk management, and a deep understanding of market behavior. While the promise of explosive gains often draws traders into the crypto space, long-term success is built on foundational principles — not on chasing pump-and-dump schemes or reacting emotionally to price swings.

The first principle is **developing a trading plan**. Every professional trader operates with a clearly defined plan that outlines entry and exit strategies, profit targets, risk tolerance, and asset selection criteria. Without this structure, traders become reactive instead of strategic — jumping into trades based on FOMO (fear of missing out) or exiting too early out of fear. A strong trading plan is your compass, especially in a market as volatile and fast-paced as crypto.

Second, every trader must understand **risk management**. The best traders aren't those who never lose — they're those who lose small and win big. Position sizing, stop-loss orders, and portfolio diversification are critical. For example, risking more than 1–2% of your portfolio on a single trade can jeopardize your long-term sustainability. Even high-conviction trades must be sized appropriately, because no strategy is 100% guaranteed.

The third foundational principle is **emotional control**. The crypto market is notorious for wild price swings, sudden crashes, and irrational hype cycles. New traders often fall into emotional traps — revenge trading after losses, panic selling during corrections, or overtrading after a win. These behaviors can destroy even the best technical strategy. Developing emotional discipline through journaling, reflection, and pre-set rules is crucial for consistent profitability.

Next, it's essential to understand **market structure and cycles**. Crypto tends to follow four key phases: accumulation, markup, distribution, and markdown. Recognizing these phases allows traders to buy when fear dominates (accumulation) and sell into strength during euphoric uptrends (markup and distribution). Understanding cycle psychology can prevent you from becoming exit liquidity when whales and institutions decide to cash out.

Another core principle is the **use of trading journals and performance tracking**. Professionals treat trading like a business, tracking every trade with notes on reasoning, outcome, and lessons learned. This habit identifies patterns in both strategy and psychology. Over time, it helps optimize your edge, showing which setups perform best and when to avoid trading altogether.

Also critical is having **clear timeframes** and selecting a trading style that fits your lifestyle. Are you a scalper, day trader, swing trader, or position trader? Scalpers make dozens of trades per day in minutes. Swing traders may hold for days or weeks. If your full-time job prevents you from watching charts all day, then short-term styles may work against you. Align your strategy with your time, temperament, and mental stamina.

Finally, it's vital to **use the right tools and platforms**. From charting software like TradingView to mobile-friendly exchanges and stop-loss automation tools, your setup can amplify your discipline. Avoid unregulated or poorly reviewed exchanges. Make sure your internet connection is reliable and have backup plans in place for outages or emergency situations.

The crypto market rewards those who are prepared, focused, and adaptive. By mastering the principles in this chapter – from planning and risk control to psychology and performance tracking – you'll build a strong foundation that elevates your chances of not just surviving, but thriving as a trader.

Cryptocurrency and Derek's story

Derek had always been fascinated by cryptocurrency. In 2018, during the height of the last bull market, he threw $5,000 into an altcoin he'd read about on Reddit. The price doubled in a week. Thrilled, he bought more. Then it tripled. "I'm a natural at this," he thought. But two weeks later, the coin crashed by 80%, and he sold in a panic — right at the bottom. He'd turned $5,000 into $15,000 and then into $2,000, all within a month. It was the perfect example of what *not* to do.

Years later, Derek sat in his home office, sipping black coffee and reviewing his trading journal. The chaotic days of emotional trading were long behind him. Now, every trade began with a plan — not a guess. His screen showed a clean layout: Fibonacci retracement levels, a 50-day moving average, and RSI plotted beneath candlesticks. Each setup had rules. Each rule had purpose.

He had learned the hard way that a trading plan wasn't optional — it was survival. Every week, he reviewed the setups that worked and those that failed. He no longer obsessed over individual wins or losses. Instead, he focused on execution quality. "Did I follow the rules?" became more important than "Did I make money?"

Derek's transformation began when he embraced risk

management. No trade risked more than 1% of his total capital. He knew that even if he lost five trades in a row, his account would be fine. Before, he had once gone all-in on a meme coin based on a friend's tweet. Now, he checked liquidity, volatility, and technical signals before every entry.

There were still temptations. Sometimes a coin would spike on Twitter hype or a breaking news alert, and the old voice would whisper: "Get in now." But Derek had rules for that too. If a coin jumped 20% in an hour without a clear breakout pattern, he let it go. Chasing pumps had never served him.

He also learned to control his emotions through journaling. After each trade, he wrote a short note: What was I feeling? Did I hesitate? Did I exit early? One week, he noticed a pattern — he often panicked out of trades too soon after two small losses. That insight helped him add a rule to hold trades until stop or target, no exceptions.

Derek wasn't glued to his screen. He had chosen swing trading, a style that fit his life. With a full-time job and two kids, he didn't have the luxury of watching the 5-minute chart all day. He analyzed on weekends and set alerts. Trading had become a business, not a casino.

His tools reflected his mindset. TradingView was his charting platform, and he used an API bot to manage stop-losses in case of sudden market crashes. He avoided shady exchanges and kept backups of all his two-factor authentication keys. A storm or power outage wouldn't leave him stranded.

Now, when people asked Derek about crypto, he didn't talk about quick gains or meme coins. He talked about plans, systems, and risk. He had learned that winning in crypto wasn't about being smarter — it was about being more disciplined.

And so, as Bitcoin's price danced on his screen, he smiled. Whether it went up or down didn't matter. He had his plan. He had his rules. He was finally trading like a pro.

Chapter 2: Technical Analysis Foundations

Technical analysis is the language of charts — a visual approach to predicting future price movements based on historical data. Unlike fundamental analysis, which evaluates a coin's intrinsic value, technical analysis focuses on price action, volume, and patterns. In a market as fast and sentiment-driven as crypto, mastering technical analysis (TA) is an essential skill for serious traders.

At the core of TA are **candlestick charts**. Each candlestick represents a period of time — such as 1 minute, 4 hours, or 1 day — and contains four pieces of information: the opening price, closing price, high, and low. A green (or white) candle means the price closed higher than it opened, while a red (or black) candle means it closed lower. These patterns allow traders to detect bullish or bearish momentum within a given timeframe.

One of the first tools traders use is **support and resistance levels**. Support is a price zone where buying pressure tends to overpower selling, causing a price bounce. Resistance is the opposite — a zone where selling outweighs buying, often leading to a price drop. These levels aren't precise numbers, but zones where price frequently reacts. Drawing horizontal lines at historical highs and lows reveals the "battle zones" where price is likely to hesitate, reverse, or break through.

Next, traders learn to identify **chart patterns**, which reflect market psychology in action. Some of the most common patterns include:

- **Triangles (ascending, descending, symmetrical)**: Consolidation patterns often followed by breakouts.
- **Head and Shoulders**: A reversal pattern that signals a shift from bullish to bearish.
- **Double Tops and Double Bottoms**: Indicate strong reversal potential.
- **Flags and Pennants**: Continuation patterns after a strong move, often followed by another surge.

Equally important are **technical indicators**, mathematical formulas applied to price data. Among the most widely used are:

- **Moving Averages (MA)**: Show average price over a period. The 50-day and 200-day moving averages are critical in identifying trend direction and crossovers.

- **Relative Strength Index (RSI)**: Measures how overbought or oversold an asset is, ranging from 0–100. A reading above 70 suggests overbought conditions; below 30 suggests oversold.

- **MACD (Moving Average Convergence Divergence)**: Combines two moving averages to signal momentum changes and possible reversals.

- **Bollinger Bands**: Display volatility based on a moving average with two standard deviations plotted above and below.

Another essential tool is **volume analysis**. Volume confirms the strength of a price move. For example, a breakout above resistance with high volume is more reliable than one on low volume. Volume spikes can also indicate accumulation or distribution by large players.

Traders also rely on **Fibonacci retracement levels**, drawn between two significant price points (like a low and a high). These levels — 23.6%, 38.2%, 50%, 61.8% — often act as support or resistance zones, where price is likely to pause or reverse.

However, the key to effective technical analysis is **confluence** — combining multiple tools to confirm a trade setup. For instance, a bullish RSI divergence at a long-term support level, combined with a bullish candlestick pattern and volume spike, may present a high-probability long entry.

Lastly, **timeframe selection** is crucial. Beginners often get whiplash from jumping between timeframes. A breakout on the 5-minute chart may be irrelevant on the 1-hour chart. Higher timeframes (daily, weekly) offer stronger signals for swing trades, while lower timeframes are better suited for intraday strategies.

Technical analysis doesn't predict the future — it improves probability. It's a skill that improves with practice, chart time, and repetition. When used properly and combined with sound risk management, TA becomes one of the most powerful tools in a trader's arsenal.

Now, let's talk about Maya's story

Maya sat in her studio apartment, her eyes glued to the screen as Bitcoin hovered just below $30,000. Her fingers hovered over the buy button, but she didn't move. Not yet. She was waiting for confirmation. Three months ago, she would have jumped in based on gut feeling or Twitter hype. Now, she waited for the chart to tell her what to do.

Her journey into technical analysis had started after losing $2,000 on an impulsive trade. She'd bought into a spike, thinking momentum would carry the price higher. Instead, it reversed within an hour. After that, she committed to learning the language of charts. She devoured books, YouTube tutorials, and courses until candlestick patterns started to make sense — like clues in a puzzle.

Now, as the price flirted with a key level, she noticed something important: the candle was forming a hammer — a potential bullish reversal pattern — right at the 61.8% Fibonacci retracement level from the recent uptrend. She glanced down. RSI was hovering at 32, indicating oversold territory. Volume had just started to spike.

That was three signs of confluence. She drew a horizontal line marking prior support. The price had bounced there twice in the past month. This wasn't guesswork anymore — this was structure. She clicked "buy" and set a stop-loss 2% below the support level. No need to watch it obsessively — she'd planned the trade and traded the plan.

Maya used TradingView as her charting software. She kept her chart simple — just candlesticks, 50- and 200-day moving averages, RSI, and volume. No clutter. Each line and indicator served a purpose. She journaled every trade, noting why she entered, what signals she saw, and how she felt at the time. She was building a feedback loop.

She remembered how confused she had been at first. Chart patterns looked arbitrary. Indicators seemed contradictory. But over time, she saw the flow — how price reacted to zones, how trends unfolded, and how whales seemed to bait retail traders with fakeouts. She learned to wait for confirmation, not just anticipation.

Maya wasn't a full-time trader. She worked a day job and traded in the evenings. But she took it seriously. She wasn't looking for a jackpot — she was building skill, one setup at a time. Some trades worked, some didn't. But she was learning to win *over time*, not just once.

That night, Bitcoin bounced hard off support, rising 5% in two hours. Her trade hit target. She didn't celebrate — just logged it, moved her stop, and closed the screen. "Another clean trade," she whispered.

Maya had come a long way. No longer at the mercy of hype or fear, she had found clarity in candlesticks, confidence in confluence, and discipline in data. Technical analysis hadn't made her rich overnight, but it had made her smarter — and that, she knew, was how real wealth began.

Chapter 3: Risk Management & Capital Protection

Risk management is the backbone of any sustainable trading strategy. While technical analysis, indicators, and entry timing often get the spotlight, it is risk management that determines whether a trader survives the ups and downs of the market. In the world of crypto, where volatility is extreme and drawdowns can be fast and deep, managing risk is not optional — it's critical.

The first key concept is **position sizing**. This refers to how much capital you allocate to a single trade. A common rule among professionals is to risk only 1% to 2% of your total portfolio on any one trade. This doesn't mean investing only 1% of your capital — it means the amount you're *willing to lose* if the trade hits your stop-loss. Proper position sizing protects your account from major losses, even if you face a series of losing trades.

Second is the **risk-reward ratio**. Every trade should be evaluated not just on the probability of success, but on the potential reward compared to the risk. A common minimum ratio is 2:1 — meaning you aim to gain twice what you risk. If you're risking $100, you should expect a profit of $200 or more. This ensures that even if only half your trades are successful, you're still growing your account over time.

Stop-loss orders are another essential tool. They define the exact price point where you'll exit a losing trade automatically. There are several types of stops:

- **Fixed percentage stop** (e.g., 2% below entry)
- **Support/resistance stop** (placed just beyond a support or resistance level)
- **ATR-based stop** (based on volatility using the Average True Range indicator)

Using stop-losses removes emotion from decision-making and enforces discipline. Never trade without one.

Conversely, **take-profit levels** should be pre-planned as well. These are the targets at which you'll lock in gains. Trailing stop-losses are useful for protecting profits as a trade moves in your favor — adjusting the stop level upward as price increases.

A crucial but overlooked element of capital protection is **avoiding over-leverage**. Many crypto exchanges offer leverage of 10x, 50x, or even 100x. While leverage can magnify profits, it also magnifies losses. A small move against you can liquidate your entire position. For new traders, using no leverage or very low leverage (2x or less) is wise until a consistent, profitable system is in place.

Diversification is another risk management strategy. Rather than putting all your funds into a single trade or asset, spread your risk across several non-correlated assets or strategies. Diversification helps reduce the impact of a single losing trade or market downturn.

Equally important is understanding **drawdowns** – the decline from a peak to a trough in your portfolio value. Accepting that losses are part of the game and planning for them mentally is key to long-term success. Smart traders manage drawdowns not by avoiding losses entirely, but by making sure no single loss is devastating.

Risk of ruin is a term from professional trading that refers to the probability of losing all your capital. The higher your risk per trade, the more likely you are to hit ruin, especially during streaks of bad luck. Risk calculators can help you understand how changes in position size affect your risk of ruin.

Lastly, **psychological discipline** is inseparable from capital protection. Even the best risk rules are useless if you override them emotionally. Fear, greed, revenge trading, and overconfidence are common traps. Building habits like journaling, taking breaks, sticking to rules, and avoiding trading when emotionally triggered will help keep your mind sharp and your capital safe.

Mastering risk management turns trading into a repeatable, professional endeavor. With the right systems, you won't fear losses — you'll understand them, limit them, and move forward stronger every time.

Lena's Ethereum trading story

Lena stared at her account balance, her heart sinking. She had just lost $4,000 in a single trade — nearly 20% of her entire portfolio — on a coin she barely researched. It wasn't the first time. The emotional rollercoaster of crypto had cost her sleep, money, and confidence. She knew something had to change.

A few weeks later, Lena was back, but this time she had a plan. She had stopped trading cold for ten days and spent that time studying risk management. No more going all-in. No more leverage roulette. She was done chasing pumps and gambling her future.

Now she opened a position in Ethereum — carefully calculated. She had $20,000 in total trading capital. She decided to risk 1% on this trade: $200. Her stop-loss was placed just under the 50-day moving average, giving the trade room to breathe while keeping her loss contained. Her target offered a 3:1 reward-to-risk ratio. This wasn't gambling anymore. It was math.

As price moved in her favor, she didn't get greedy. She moved her stop-loss up to breakeven, letting the trade run without fear. Eventually, her take-profit level hit, and the trade closed — a clean $600 gain. It felt better than any moonshot win because it was earned through discipline.

But her real growth came weeks later, during a losing streak. Three trades in a row hit stop-loss. Old Lena would have doubled down or switched strategies mid-trade. The new Lena stuck to her plan. Each loss was small — just $200 each — and she didn't deviate. Because she knew: no system wins every time. Survival was the goal.

She used a spreadsheet to track her trades and another to calculate position sizes automatically based on risk and stop-loss distance. She even created a rulebook for herself: Never risk more than 1%. No trading before coffee. No doubling down. Take breaks after losses. Celebrate process, not outcomes.

The most liberating change came when she stopped using high leverage. She remembered being wiped out in 30 seconds on a 10x leveraged trade. Now, she used 1x — or occasionally 2x —

and only with ironclad setups. Her account no longer looked like a rollercoaster graph.

She diversified too. Some capital stayed in stablecoins earning interest. Some went into swing trades. A small portion was allocated to long-term holds. Even if one strategy had a bad week, her entire portfolio stayed healthy.

Months later, Lena's account had grown, but more importantly — her confidence had returned. Not the overconfidence of her earlier days, but a grounded, quiet kind. The kind that comes from knowing you're protected, that you're not betting your future on luck.

Crypto was still wild, but she wasn't. She had become her own shield — with rules, math, patience, and discipline. And that made all the difference.

Chapter 4: Pro Tools and Platforms for Crypto Trading

Successful crypto trading isn't just about strategy — it's about having the right tools to execute that strategy efficiently and securely. While many beginners stick to basic exchange apps or mobile wallets, advanced traders leverage a range of professional platforms, tools, and data sources to gain an edge. In this chapter, we'll explore the best tools across five key categories: charting, execution, automation, analysis, and risk control.

The foundation of all analysis begins with **charting platforms**. Among them, **TradingView** is the gold standard. It allows traders to chart thousands of assets across multiple exchanges using powerful technical indicators, drawing tools, and multi-timeframe analysis. Users can create custom scripts with Pine Script, set alerts, publish strategies, and even integrate with brokers. TradingView also offers social features where traders share setups and strategies — great for idea validation and learning.

For on-chain data, **CryptoQuant** and **Glassnode** offer institutional-grade analytics. They provide insights like exchange inflows/outflows, miner activity, whale accumulation, and stablecoin supply metrics. These metrics help traders predict potential price movements and understand market sentiment beyond charts.

When it comes to trade execution, the choice of **exchange** is critical. Professional traders prioritize **security, liquidity, and reliability**. Top centralized exchanges (CEXs) include **Binance**, **Kraken**, **Coinbase Pro**, and **Bybit**. These platforms offer spot trading, margin accounts, futures, and options. Each has pros and cons in terms of fees, interface, and supported pairs. For U.S. traders, regulation-compliant platforms are essential.

However, decentralized exchanges (DEXs) like **Uniswap**, **SushiSwap**, and **dYdX** are gaining popularity among serious traders for their non-custodial nature. Using DEXs requires wallet integration and an understanding of slippage, gas fees, and liquidity pools — but they provide transparency and control unmatched by centralized options.

Advanced traders often incorporate **automation tools** like **3Commas**, **Pionex**, and **TradeSanta**, which offer customizable trading bots. These tools allow for grid trading, DCA (dollar cost averaging), and trailing stop strategies. Some bots integrate directly with exchanges through APIs and can be backtested using historical data before deploying real capital.

For users who prefer building their own tools, platforms like

MetaTrader 5, **Shrimpy**, or **Cryptohopper** provide API support, signal-based automation, and portfolio tracking features. Traders can code algorithms or subscribe to third-party strategies, which opens the door to semi-passive trading.

A powerful tool in the trader's arsenal is **backtesting software**. Platforms like **TradingView's Strategy Tester**, **CoinMarketMan**, and **QuantConnect** allow you to simulate trades based on historical data to evaluate performance. Proper backtesting helps avoid "curve fitting" and gives you data-driven confidence in your strategy.

For real-time news and alerts, **Twitter**, **Telegram channels**, and apps like **CryptoPanic** or **CoinDesk** are critical. Fast access to news can help you react before the market does – especially for major events like exchange hacks, regulatory news, or sudden whale transfers.

Portfolio and performance tracking is equally important. Tools like **CoinStats**, **Delta**, or **Zerion** help monitor holdings across wallets and exchanges. They allow you to visualize gains, losses, and asset allocation, all while syncing automatically with wallets and APIs.

Security tools like **Ledger**, **Trezor**, and **YubiKey** are essential for capital protection. Use hardware wallets for storage and hardware authentication for logins. Never store large sums on exchanges, and enable two-factor authentication (2FA) wherever possible.

In summary, professional trading requires a suite of tools working in harmony — from data analysis to execution, automation, and security. Your setup should enhance clarity, reduce manual errors, and streamline decision-making. As your skill level and capital grow, so too should your infrastructure. Equip yourself well, and the results will reflect it.

How Ethan mastered the process

Ethan had always been a hands-on trader — the kind who made every decision manually. He'd wake up early, scroll through charts, and place orders directly on his exchange's web app. It worked at first — until the market sped up, his portfolio grew, and his life got busier. He missed opportunities, made rushed decisions, and more than once, forgot to set a stop-loss.

It was a stressful way to trade.

One day, after missing a massive breakout on Chainlink because he was in traffic and couldn't access his account,

Ethan made a decision: it was time to upgrade. No more relying on mobile apps and hunches. He was going pro.

His first move was switching his charts to **TradingView**. It was a revelation. The clean interface, endless indicators, and ability to save multiple layout profiles gave him a sense of control he never had. He set alerts, drew Fibonacci levels, and even learned a bit of Pine Script to automate some signals. For the first time, he felt like the charts were speaking to him in a language he could understand.

Next, he opened accounts with multiple **exchanges**. While he kept some funds on **Kraken** for fiat on-ramps, he started using **Bybit** for low-fee, high-liquidity altcoin trades. He learned how to route trades efficiently, how to use post-only orders to save fees, and how to manage slippage during volatile moves.

But Ethan didn't stop there. He set up a **3Commas** account and experimented with trading bots. He created a simple DCA bot that bought Ethereum during dips. It wasn't flashy, but it was consistent — and it worked while he was asleep or working. He backtested the strategy using **TradingView's Strategy Tester**, refining the entries based on RSI and moving average confluence. His win rate improved, but more importantly, he gained confidence in his system.

He also began using **Glassnode**. He was fascinated by on-chain metrics — like Bitcoin's exchange reserves, miner net position change, and whale wallet activity. He started spotting subtle shifts in sentiment long before retail traders reacted. One time, he exited a major altcoin position hours before a 15% drop, simply because of abnormal exchange inflows he saw on CryptoQuant.

To stay ahead of news, Ethan built a dashboard with **CryptoPanic**, hooked into his Twitter feed, and joined Telegram alert channels for top traders. The first time he caught a pump before the news hit CoinMarketCap, he felt like a professional — no longer reacting, but anticipating.

He also bought a **Ledger Nano X** and migrated 80% of his long-term holdings to cold storage. He used **YubiKey** for 2FA and started using VPNs when trading in public places. After hearing about too many SIM-swap and phishing attacks, he knew: no strategy mattered if his security was weak.

By the end of the quarter, Ethan's results were more consistent than ever. His trades were structured, his tools worked in sync, and his stress had dropped dramatically. Trading had become scalable, even enjoyable. He wasn't glued to the screen — because the tools were doing their job.

Looking back, he realized something: professional trading wasn't just about mastering the market. It was about mastering *your setup*. The right tools didn't just make him faster — they made him smarter, safer, and more in control. And that's what made the real difference.

Chapter 5: Chart Patterns, Breakouts & Fakeouts

In technical trading, **chart patterns** serve as visual footprints of market psychology. They reflect the collective decisions of buyers and sellers and can indicate potential reversals, continuations, or indecision. But while patterns can be powerful tools for anticipating price movement, they also carry the risk of **fakeouts** — false breakouts that trap unsuspecting traders. Mastering this chapter means learning to distinguish real moves from deception.

The most common patterns fall into three categories: **reversal patterns, continuation patterns**, and **indecision patterns**.

Among reversal patterns, **Head and Shoulders** is one of the most reliable. It features three peaks: a higher middle peak (head) between two lower highs (shoulders). When price breaks the "neckline" (support level), it often signals the end of an uptrend. Its inverse — the **Inverse Head and Shoulders** — is a bullish reversal at the bottom of a downtrend.

Double Tops and **Double Bottoms** are also key reversal signals. A double top looks like an "M" and indicates that price failed twice to break a resistance level. A double bottom resembles a “W” and signals that buyers defended a support level twice. These patterns gain credibility with rising volume on the breakout.

Continuation patterns suggest the prevailing trend will resume. The most common are:

- **Triangles** (ascending, descending, symmetrical): These indicate a tightening range and eventual breakout. Ascending triangles often break upward; descending triangles tend to break downward.

- **Flags** and **Pennants**: Small consolidations after strong price moves. Flags slope against the trend, while pennants are more symmetrical. Breakouts typically follow in the direction of the original move.

- **Cup and Handle**: A bullish continuation pattern. The “cup” is a rounded bottom, and the “handle” is a small pullback before breakout.

Rectangles and **wedges** can act as either continuation or reversal patterns, depending on the direction of the breakout.

Identifying **breakouts** is essential. A breakout occurs when price closes beyond a key support or resistance level. However, successful breakout trading requires confirmation. Watch for:

- **Volume spike**: Higher volume confirms that the breakout is supported by strong participation.
- **Retest of the broken level**: Price breaks out, pulls back to the breakout level, and then continues. This increases the probability that the breakout is real.

But not all breakouts are trustworthy. Many are **fakeouts** — moves that temporarily break a key level, only to reverse quickly. Fakeouts often occur during low volume periods, news events, or when stop-loss clusters are targeted.

To avoid fakeouts, consider these tips:

1. **Wait for candle closes**: Don't act on intrabar price action; wait for confirmation on the timeframe you're trading.
2. **Check higher timeframes**: A breakout on the 15-minute chart may be irrelevant on the 4-hour or daily chart.
3. **Look for confluence**: Combine chart patterns with indicators like RSI divergence, volume trends, or moving averages.
4. **Use stop-loss discipline**: Place stops in logical areas — not too tight that normal fluctuations stop you out,

but not so loose that you risk unnecessary losses.

Advanced traders also watch for **liquidity grabs** – when price intentionally breaches a level to trigger stop-losses before reversing. This is common around psychologically important zones like round numbers ($1.00, $10,000, etc.). Whale traders often use fakeouts to accumulate positions before launching the real move.

Patterns and breakouts work best in **liquid markets** with strong trends. They're less reliable in sideways, choppy conditions. Practice and screen time are essential. Every pattern is unique in shape, context, and market condition. No pattern guarantees success – but when understood and confirmed properly, they offer a significant edge.

How Nico overcame his fear of fakeouts

Nico had been staring at the chart for nearly an hour. Solana had formed a textbook ascending triangle. Each pullback found support at a flat base, while the highs kept getting tighter. He'd drawn the resistance line weeks ago. And now, the price hovered just beneath it, like a rocket ready to launch.

He could feel his pulse rising.

The last time he saw a similar pattern, he jumped in too soon – only to watch the price break out for two minutes, reverse hard, and wipe out his position. That experience had left a scar, but it also taught him discipline.

This time, Nico waited.

He zoomed out to the 4-hour chart. The trend was up. RSI was climbing, but not yet overbought. Volume was slowly building. Then it happened — a large green candle surged above resistance, closing solidly on increased volume. It wasn't a wick. It was a close. That was his signal.

He entered with half his position. No full bets until confirmation. He set his stop-loss just below the triangle's base and placed an alert for a potential retest.

Sure enough, price pulled back. Many traders panicked. Nico didn't. The pullback landed perfectly on the broken resistance — now acting as support. It held. The next candle was green. He entered the second half of his position and tightened his stop.

Over the next two days, Solana rallied 18%. But Nico wasn't riding just momentum — he was following a structure. It felt calm. Controlled.

A few weeks later, he faced the opposite situation. Cardano was forming what looked like an inverse head and shoulders — but something felt off. Volume was declining. RSI showed bearish divergence. Still, Twitter was buzzing: "ADA to the moon!" Even some influencers were calling it the "next breakout."

Tempted but cautious, Nico waited for the neckline to break. It did — barely — but without volume. The next candle reversed hard. It was a **fakeout**. The pattern had lured in hopeful traders, only to trap them in losses. Nico watched from the sidelines, glad he'd waited.

He started building a personal "pattern journal," screenshotting every triangle, double top, and flag he saw. He noted the volume, context, and result. Over time, patterns became more than shapes — they became stories. He could read the crowd's emotions in the chart. He saw where traders felt fear, where they got greedy, and where the smart money stepped in.

His breakthrough came when he began pairing patterns with other tools. If RSI divergence lined up with a triangle breakout, he paid attention. If Bollinger Bands were squeezing tight before a flag pattern, he knew volatility was coming. He stopped trading every setup and began waiting for *great* setups.

Nico no longer feared fakeouts. He expected them, planned for them, and used them to learn. Breakouts were no longer adrenaline rushes. They were calculated moments in a longer game — one that he was finally learning to play with skill, not just luck.

Chapter 6: Using Indicators Like a Pro

Technical indicators are the power tools of advanced crypto traders. While chart patterns and support/resistance levels offer valuable insights, indicators provide quantitative, repeatable data to help confirm trends, reversals, and momentum shifts. However, using too many indicators — or using them incorrectly — can lead to confusion and contradictory signals. The key is **selective mastery**: understanding a handful of indicators deeply and using them in combination to build confluence.

One of the most widely used tools is the **Relative Strength Index (RSI)**. RSI measures the speed and change of price movements, oscillating between 0 and 100. Traditionally, a value above 70 signals overbought conditions, while below 30 indicates oversold territory. However, RSI can remain in these zones for extended periods during strong trends. What's more valuable are **divergences** — when price makes a higher high but RSI makes a lower high (bearish divergence), or vice versa (bullish divergence). These divergences often precede reversals.

Next is **Moving Averages (MA)** — specifically, the **Simple Moving Average (SMA)** and **Exponential Moving Average (EMA)**. Moving averages help smooth out price data to identify trend direction. The 50-day and 200-day SMAs are commonly used for swing trading and trend identification. **Golden crosses** (when the 50-day crosses above the 200-day) and **death crosses** (when it crosses below) are considered powerful trend signals. EMAs give more weight to recent price action and are often used for faster decisions — especially on intraday charts.

The **Moving Average Convergence Divergence (MACD)** is a momentum indicator made of two EMAs and a histogram. The MACD line crossing above the signal line generates a bullish signal, while crossing below indicates bearish momentum. Traders watch for MACD crossovers and the zero line for confirmation. Like RSI, **MACD divergence** can also be a strong predictor of trend reversal.

Another key indicator is **Bollinger Bands**. These bands consist of a moving average and two standard deviation lines (one above and one below). When price touches or breaks the outer bands, it often signals increased volatility and potential reversals. However, in trending markets, price can ride the outer band for extended periods. A **Bollinger Band squeeze** — when the bands contract tightly — signals an upcoming breakout, although direction must be confirmed by other tools.

Volume indicators are crucial for validating breakouts and patterns. The **Volume Oscillator** or **On-Balance Volume (OBV)** tracks cumulative buying and selling pressure. A breakout with strong volume is more likely to succeed than one on low volume. Conversely, falling volume on a rally may indicate a weakening trend.

For traders who want to measure volatility directly, the **Average True Range (ATR)** is essential. ATR doesn't indicate trend direction, but shows how much an asset typically moves over a given time period. Traders use ATR to set stop-loss distances and adjust position sizing based on expected volatility.

Advanced traders also use **Ichimoku Cloud**, a multi-line indicator that combines support, resistance, trend direction, and momentum in one view. The cloud (Kumo) helps identify whether price is in bullish or bearish territory, while crossovers between the conversion line (Tenkan-sen) and base line (Kijun-sen) offer entry and exit signals. Though complex at first, Ichimoku is highly effective when mastered.

But none of these tools should be used in isolation. Indicators work best when confirming each other. For example, a bullish MACD crossover combined with a bounce off the 50-day EMA and a bullish RSI divergence offers a high-probability setup.

This **confluence** gives the trader confidence to execute without hesitation.

Lastly, avoid **indicator overload**. Too many signals can contradict and paralyze decision-making. Instead, build a minimalist dashboard — 3 to 5 core indicators that you understand thoroughly. Use backtesting to validate combinations that suit your trading style and timeframe.

Indicators are not crystal balls — they're tools to interpret probability. Used wisely, they elevate your trading from guesswork to precision.

How Tasha learned to use RSI, EMA, MACD

Tasha loved data. As a former math teacher turned full-time crypto trader, numbers comforted her. Patterns intrigued her. But when she first entered the world of indicators, she was overwhelmed. Her charts looked like a rainbow spaghetti of lines — MACD, RSI, Bollinger Bands, Fibonacci levels, stochastic, parabolic SAR — all stacked on top of each other. It felt like progress, but in truth, it was chaos.

Her breakthrough came when she stripped everything away and started fresh.

She decided to focus on just **three indicators**: RSI, EMA, and MACD. She studied them like sacred texts. Every day, she reviewed how each behaved in different conditions – uptrends, consolidations, false breakouts. She began seeing patterns. RSI divergence before price reversals. MACD crossovers predicting momentum shifts. The 21 EMA acting like a magnetic support in strong uptrends.

She remembered one specific trade on MATIC. The coin had been consolidating for days. Price touched the lower Bollinger Band just as RSI dipped to 29. MACD hadn't crossed yet — but was curling up. She placed a small long position, just to test her thesis. Two days later, MACD crossed bullish, RSI climbed above 40, and price surged 15%. It was the first time she felt like she *read* the chart instead of guessing.

Tasha's new strategy focused on **confluence**. She wouldn't act on a single signal. RSI alone wasn't enough. She needed two or more indicators to confirm the setup. A MACD crossover wasn't a trigger unless volume supported the move or RSI divergence appeared.

She even created what she called her "Confidence Checklist":

- RSI divergence on 4-hour or daily chart?
- MACD crossing above signal line?
- Price above 50 EMA?

- Breakout volume higher than previous 3 candles?
- Any candlestick reversal patterns near support?

If she could check at least three of the five, she would enter a trade. Otherwise, she passed.

Her trading improved dramatically. She no longer reacted emotionally to green or red candles. She waited for setups to build. Some days, she didn't trade at all – and that was okay. She journaled every entry, noting what indicators aligned and what the outcome was.

Tasha also began using **ATR** to size her trades. If volatility was high, she reduced her position. If ATR was low, she increased size slightly but kept stops tight. It brought balance to her strategy.

One day, a friend asked her, "How do you know when to trust an indicator?" She smiled. "I don't trust indicators. I trust what they're telling me *together*."

She kept her charts clean now – just price, volume, MACD, RSI, and a couple of EMAs. The simplicity gave her clarity. She no longer needed to predict. She just had to *read* what the market was already showing.

Indicators didn't make her perfect. She still had losing trades. But she now had a system, backed by logic, probability, and a calm mind. And for Tasha, that was the real win.

Chapter 7: Entry & Exit Strategies That Win

The difference between an average trader and a consistently profitable one often lies not in spotting opportunities, but in executing precise **entry and exit strategies**. Knowing *when* to enter a trade and *how* to exit — whether in profit or loss — is what separates emotion-driven guesses from data-backed decisions. This chapter will equip you with the core techniques used by advanced traders to improve timing, maximize gains, and cut losses with discipline.

A successful **entry strategy** starts with **context**. Are you trading in a trending market or a consolidating range? Are you trading the trend, fading it, or attempting a breakout? The answer informs your entry method.

In trending markets, entries are typically made on **pullbacks to dynamic support** such as the 21 EMA or 50 EMA. In consolidations, traders often enter at the range extremes — buying support and selling resistance — or waiting for a confirmed breakout with a retest. Either way, the entry must be **planned**, not impulsive.

One of the most reliable methods for entries is **breakout with retest**. Instead of entering on the first candle that breaches resistance, traders wait for a **retest** of the broken level, confirming it as new support. This adds confluence and reduces the risk of entering a fakeout.

Another method is **limit order placement** at predefined zones. This is common when trading Fibonacci retracement levels, order blocks, or previous high/low zones. Limit orders allow for favorable pricing but require precision and trust in your analysis.

Advanced traders also use **confirmation entries**, waiting for indicators to align. For instance, they may enter long only when RSI is rising, MACD has crossed bullish, and price has reclaimed a moving average. These traders sacrifice early entries for increased probability.

Now let's talk about **exit strategies** – arguably the most neglected skill among traders. A profitable trade can turn into a loser without a proper exit plan. Exits fall into three categories:

1. **Take-Profit Exits**: Pre-defined price levels where you secure your gains.
2. **Trailing Stop Exits**: Dynamically adjust your stop-loss upward as the price moves in your favor.

3. **Signal-Based Exits**: Closing trades when indicators flip or reversal patterns form.

A **take-profit** level should be based on nearby resistance levels, Fibonacci extensions, or measured moves (e.g., the height of a triangle pattern projected forward). Using a 2:1 or 3:1 reward-to-risk ratio ensures long-term profitability, even if your win rate is 50%.

Trailing stops allow you to let winners run while protecting profits. Some traders trail using moving averages (e.g., 21 EMA), ATR multiples, or fixed percentages. Others move their stop to breakeven after price hits the first take-profit level.

Signal-based exits use technical indicators such as MACD crossing bearish, RSI divergence, or candle patterns like bearish engulfing. While these are dynamic, they require constant monitoring and fast execution.

A hybrid approach often works best — taking partial profit at a set target and letting the rest ride with a trailing stop. This way, you lock in gains and leave room for upside. Some traders exit in stages: 50% at the first target, 25% at the second, and let the final 25% trail.

Lastly, **exit discipline during losing trades** is vital. Never move your stop-loss wider once a trade is in motion. Respect your risk management plan. Getting stopped out is part of the game. What matters is staying in the game.

Entries and exits are not standalone events — they are part of a **complete trade plan** that also includes position sizing and risk controls. The more repeatable your entry and exit strategies are, the more consistent your results will be.

Ajun's exit strategy

Arjun had always been good at spotting trades. He could glance at a chart and see potential. But for some reason, his account was stuck — not growing, not shrinking, just going in circles. It wasn't until he reviewed his journal that he saw the pattern: bad timing on entries, and even worse timing on exits.

"I get in too early or too late," he admitted to himself. "And I never know when to get out."

Determined to change that, he rewired his strategy. His first move was to abandon market orders entirely. He began planning **limit entries**, placing buy orders at support zones and retracement levels, rather than chasing candles mid-flight. One trade on Avalanche taught him everything.

Price was breaking out above resistance — everyone was jumping in. Arjun wanted to buy too, but paused. He marked the breakout level, placed a limit buy just below it, and waited for a retest. Hours later, the price dipped, tagged his order, and then soared. The entry gave him a better price and more confidence.

His exit strategy needed even more work. Before, he would either close the whole trade in panic when price wobbled or get greedy and hold too long. Now, he used **measured targets** based on chart patterns. If he traded a flag, he projected the flagpole height forward to calculate a take-profit zone.

He also added **trailing stops** to his system. On a Cardano trade, once price moved up 8%, he moved his stop to breakeven. When it hit 12%, he trailed his stop just below the 21 EMA. Price continued rising. He eventually exited with a 20% gain — his best trade in months — and it felt effortless.

Another change was **partial exits**. He stopped treating every trade as all-or-nothing. Instead, he took 50% profit at his first target, let 25% go to a secondary target, and trailed the rest. It was freeing. Even when the final portion stopped out early, he still locked in a win.

But his proudest moment came during a loss.

He entered a trade on LINK that looked promising, but it started to stall. His stop-loss was 2% below entry. Price dipped slowly... then tagged it. He was tempted to widen the stop —

"It might bounce!" — but he didn't. He let it go. He lost 2%. But the old Arjun would've turned that into 10%.

He smiled as he logged the loss. "Perfect exit," he wrote.

With his new rules, trading felt less emotional. He had a plan before each trade. He knew his entry trigger, his stop, his targets. It wasn't about guessing anymore. It was about executing.

Arjun no longer feared missing out or being wrong. He just focused on the next clean setup — because now, he had a system that told him exactly when to get in... and more importantly, when to get out.

Chapter 8: Psychology of High-Performance Trading

Mastering charts, indicators, and risk strategies is vital – but even the most advanced systems fall apart without the right **trader psychology**. Your mindset is the lens through which you interpret data, react to wins and losses, and maintain discipline. In high-performance trading, psychological strength is what turns consistency into profitability.

The first pillar of trading psychology is **emotional regulation**. Fear and greed are the twin forces that sabotage even the most rational strategies. Fear causes hesitation, early exits, and missed opportunities. Greed leads to overtrading, revenge trading, and oversized positions. The most successful traders are emotionally neutral – calm in wins, detached in losses, and focused on the process over the outcome.

To reach this level, traders must build **self-awareness**. Keeping a **trading journal** is one of the most effective tools for this. Record every trade, the reason behind it, how you felt before entering, what happened after, and how you responded. Over time, this builds a mirror into your behavior and reveals patterns. You'll begin to notice habits – like impulsive trades after a win, or a tendency to move stop-losses when feeling uncertain.

Another core principle is developing a **rules-based mindset**. This means relying on pre-defined systems, not emotions or gut instincts. A system tells you *when to trade, when not to*, and exactly what to do in every situation. Without rules, you are guessing — and the markets punish guesswork. With rules, you are following a structured process that can be refined over time.

Discipline is the muscle that enforces your rules. It's easy to follow your plan when everything is going well — but the real test is during drawdowns, news volatility, or unexpected losses. High-performance traders accept losses as part of the game. They don't fight the market or try to "make it back." They stick to their edge and let the probabilities play out.

Equally important is your **belief system** around money. Many traders subconsciously sabotage themselves because of deep-seated beliefs: "I don't deserve to make this much," "Money is hard to earn," or "I always lose when I try something new." Identifying and replacing these limiting beliefs with empowering ones — like "I manage risk like a pro," or "My edge plays out over time" — changes your internal narrative and boosts your confidence.

Routine and rituals also contribute to trading success. Start each day with a pre-market ritual: review charts, plan your trades, meditate, or review affirmations. End your day with a post-market ritual: review results, journal, and step away from the screens. This creates structure and separates trading from the rest of your life, reducing emotional bleed-over.

High-level traders also avoid **identity-based trading**. They don't let wins inflate their ego or losses destroy their confidence. They don't need to "prove" themselves with every trade. They see themselves as process-driven practitioners — more like surgeons than gamblers.

Lastly, understand the concept of **mental capital**. Just like financial capital, your ability to make sound decisions is finite. Avoid decision fatigue by limiting how many trades you take, scheduling breaks, and staying away from the charts after emotional trades.

Psychology is not a one-time fix. It is a continuous discipline, much like physical training. The stronger your mind becomes, the more precise and profitable your trading decisions will be.

Now, let's talk about Diego.

Diego had all the tools. His charts were pristine, his indicators dialed in, his risk management on point. Yet, week after week, something went wrong. He would enter early, exit too late, double down on losses. He once turned a winning week into a losing month because he couldn't stop revenge trading after a stop-loss got hit by a single candle wick.

It wasn't his system that was broken. It was *him*.

One afternoon, after closing his laptop in frustration, he took a walk and asked himself the question that changed everything: "What if the problem isn't the market... but my mind?"

The next morning, Diego began a new practice: a **trading journal**. But not just numbers — emotions. For every trade, he wrote what he was feeling, what his inner voice was saying. At first, it felt silly. But within two weeks, patterns emerged. He noticed that after every win, he felt invincible and traded too much. After losses, he'd get tense, skip confirmations, and enter on impulse.

His journal became a mirror, and the reflection was honest.

He started building **rules** — not for strategy, but for behavior. "No trading after two consecutive losses." "If I feel FOMO, I wait two candles." "Only trade the first two hours of my chosen sessions." He posted these rules on his wall. When he broke them, he didn't shame himself. He reviewed, learned, and adjusted.

One day, he hit three losses in a row. Old Diego would've kept trading to "win it back." New Diego closed his charts, went for a run, and came back the next day with a clear head. That alone saved him thousands.

But it wasn't just discipline. Diego also worked on his **beliefs about money**. He realized he had grown up hearing that "rich people are lucky" and "easy money doesn't last." Subconsciously, he'd been sabotaging profits, exiting early, or adding stress where it wasn't needed. He replaced those beliefs with new affirmations: "I earn through skill," "Discipline creates wealth," "I protect both capital and mindset."

He created **rituals** – five minutes of meditation before each session, a glass of water, reviewing the plan, deep breath. It centered him. He stopped needing to be right. He just needed to follow the plan. Win or lose, it was about execution.

As months passed, Diego didn't become emotionless – he became **emotionally aware**. He knew when to step back, when to push forward, and when to simply walk away. He wasn't perfect, but he was consistent. And that changed everything.

Now, when people asked him the secret to success, he didn't talk about indicators or setups. He smiled and said, "The real game? It's all in your head."

Chapter 9: Building and Backtesting a Winning Strategy

A winning trading strategy isn't a secret signal or a magic indicator — it's a structured system of rules designed to give you a **statistical edge** over time. Professional traders don't rely on hope or instinct. They **build, test, and refine** their strategies using real data before ever risking capital. This chapter shows you how to develop a personalized trading strategy and how to validate it using backtesting methods to ensure long-term consistency and profitability.

The first step is **defining your trading style**. Are you a day trader, swing trader, or position trader? Your strategy must align with your time availability, psychology, and risk tolerance. A scalper will need precise, rapid-fire setups on low timeframes. A swing trader may operate off the 4-hour or daily chart and hold for days. There's no "right" style — only the one that fits you.

Next, create a **framework for your system**, which includes:

1. **Market conditions**: Does the strategy work in trending, ranging, or volatile markets?
2. **Entry criteria**: What exact signals must align before you enter? (e.g., bullish RSI divergence, MACD

crossover, breakout from triangle, etc.)

3. **Stop-loss placement**: Where will you exit if the trade goes against you?

4. **Take-profit method**: Will you target a fixed R:R (reward-to-risk) ratio, use Fibonacci extensions, or trail stops?

5. **Indicators and filters**: Which tools will you use to filter out bad setups?

6. **Position sizing**: How much will you risk per trade?

Once this structure is in place, the next step is **backtesting** – the process of applying your strategy to historical data to see how it would have performed. This provides insight into the system's **win rate, average reward-to-risk ratio, drawdowns**, and profitability.

Manual backtesting involves going through past charts and logging each setup as if you were trading it live. For each setup, you document entry, stop-loss, take-profit, and outcome. This can be done in TradingView using the bar replay feature.

Automated backtesting uses platforms like:

- **TradingView's Strategy Tester** (with Pine Script)

- **QuantConnect** (Python-based strategy engine)
- **Backtrader** (for algorithmic strategy testing)
- **CryptoTester** or **Chartlog** (for discretionary traders)

During backtesting, track key metrics:

- **Win rate**: Percentage of profitable trades.
- **Profit factor**: Gross profit divided by gross loss (a PF > 1.5 is generally good).
- **Maximum drawdown**: The largest peak-to-trough loss — reveals how risky the system is.
- **Average R:R**: The mean ratio of reward to risk per trade.
- **Expectancy**: The average profit per trade considering win rate and R:R.

After backtesting, **forward testing** comes next. This means applying the strategy in real-time (on a demo or small live account) to see how it performs in actual market conditions, including slippage, execution speed, and news impact.

It's also critical to document and **refine** your strategy over time. Many traders use **Notion**, **Google Sheets**, or dedicated trade journals to log data, spot recurring issues, and improve setups. This creates a feedback loop where each trade becomes an input to a better strategy.

Lastly, accept that no system works 100% of the time. Even a strong strategy can have losing streaks. The goal isn't perfection — it's **consistency, clarity, and control**. Backtesting doesn't eliminate risk, but it helps you understand and manage it with confidence.

Building and backtesting a strategy transforms trading from speculation to structured decision-making. It's the foundation of every professional trader's career — and the beginning of true mastery.

Why Mina chose swing trading

Mina had tried everything. YouTube strategies, paid signals, Reddit tips — nothing worked for long. One week she'd be up, the next down twice as much. She was tired of bouncing between gurus and guessing games. One night, after another painful loss, she closed her laptop and muttered, "I need a *real* plan."

The next day, she started building her own trading strategy. No more copying others. It was going to be hers — tested, tracked, and tailored to how *she* thinks and trades.

First, she defined her style. Mina had a full-time job, so day trading was out. She chose **swing trading** on the 4-hour chart — slow enough to manage, fast enough for consistent trades. She decided to focus on trend continuation setups, using RSI, MACD, and Fibonacci retracements.

She mapped out her rules:

- Trade only in uptrending markets.
- Enter on a pullback to the 61.8% Fibonacci level, confirmed by RSI oversold and a MACD curl.
- Stop-loss just below the swing low.
- Take profit at the recent high or use a 2.5:1 R:R ratio.
- Risk 1.5% per trade.

With her plan on paper, she opened TradingView and began **manual backtesting** the past six months of Ethereum data. She used the bar replay tool to simulate the market candle by candle. Every time her setup appeared, she logged the trade — entry, stop, target, and outcome — into Google Sheets.

After 40 sample trades, her results were encouraging:

- Win rate: 55%

- Average R:R: 2.2:1
- Profit factor: 1.8
- Maximum drawdown: 8%
- Expectancy: Positive

It wasn't magic. It was data. And it changed everything.

She began **forward testing** her strategy with $100 trades. It wasn't about making money yet — it was about building confidence. She discovered real-world issues: slippage during news events, hesitation in live trades, missed setups while sleeping. She adjusted her alerts and added time filters to trade only between 6 AM and 10 PM.

Each weekend, she reviewed her trades like a coach studying game tape. She spotted flaws. One trade she took on a weekend pump was outside her plan — she removed weekend trading from her strategy. Another entry happened too soon — she added a candle close confirmation rule.

Mina's journal filled with screenshots, notes, and lessons. Her strategy evolved — not wildly, but through small, data-driven tweaks. She stopped chasing trades. She waited. She planned. And most importantly, she believed in her system.

One day, a friend asked, "How do you know it'll work?"

She smiled and replied, "Because I've *seen* it work. Over 50 trades. It's not perfect — but it's mine."

From chaos to control, Mina had built something few traders ever do — a strategy that fit her life, worked with her psychology, and was proven by her own two hands.

And in that structure, she found freedom.

Chapter 10: Scaling and Automating Your Trading System

Once you've built a proven, profitable trading strategy, the next evolution is **scaling** and **automating** your system. Scaling increases your profits without proportionally increasing risk or time spent. Automation reduces emotional interference, increases consistency, and allows you to trade even when you're not physically present. In this chapter, we'll cover how advanced traders level up using position scaling, capital allocation models, automation tools, and passive management workflows.

Scaling Starts With Capital Efficiency

Before scaling up your trade size, you must first confirm **statistical reliability**. That means a strategy with:

- At least 30–50 backtested trades,
- A positive profit factor (1.5+),
- Reasonable drawdowns (preferably under 20%),
- And a clearly defined edge.

From there, you can scale in two ways: **position size growth** and **position scaling into trades**.

- **Position size growth** means increasing your risk per trade — from 1% to 1.5%, then to 2%, while maintaining discipline.
- **Position scaling** refers to entering a position in stages — buying 33% at the first signal, 33% on confirmation, and 33% after a breakout. This smooths entry risk and often improves your average entry price.

Traders can also **scale out of trades** by exiting in stages. This locks in gains while allowing upside to run, creating a compounding effect on equity growth.

Capital Allocation Strategies

As your portfolio grows, not all your capital needs to be active. Many pro traders segment funds into:

- **Core strategy allocation** (e.g., swing trading)
- **Passive long-term holds**
- **Stablecoin interest accounts**
- **Algorithmic or bot-assisted trades**
- **Experimental high-risk trades** (with small allocation)

Using **Kelly Criterion** or **Fixed Fractional Models** allows you to determine the optimal portion of capital to risk per trade to maximize growth without overexposing yourself.

Automating Execution and Management

Automation in trading isn't just about bots — it's about systems. It can include:

- **Trade alerts and triggers**
- **Automatic stop-loss and take-profit settings**
- **Trailing stops**
- **Portfolio rebalancing tools**
- **API-based trading bots**

Platforms like **3Commas**, **Pionex**, **TradeSanta**, and **Cryptohopper** allow rule-based bot setups for trend following, DCA, grid trading, and scalping. More advanced users build on **MetaTrader**, **QuantConnect**, or **TradingView's Pine Script** for custom scripts that execute trades automatically based on strategy logic.

Bots don't guarantee profits. Their power lies in **removing emotion** and ensuring rules are followed without hesitation.

Systemizing Your Workflow

To become scalable, treat trading like a business:

- Set up a **weekly trade planning ritual** (scanning setups, setting alerts, refining strategy).
- Use a **project management tool** (like Notion or Trello) to track performance and ideas.
- Create **templates** for trade journaling, analysis, and weekly reviews.

Build your own **dashboard** using Excel, Google Sheets, or dedicated trade management software. Include performance metrics, equity curve, and trade breakdowns to improve clarity.

Also consider **automating your life around trading** – from syncing market schedules to alerts on your phone and cloud backups for your data. Automation frees your mental energy for critical decisions.

Scaling With Discipline

Finally, understand that growth must be matched with mindset. More capital = more pressure. Don't jump from trading $500 per position to $5,000 overnight. Slowly increase exposure as you adapt emotionally and operationally.

Set **scaling checkpoints** – only increase size after 20 consecutive trades with consistent execution. Focus on *execution*, not just profits.

Scaling and automation are not about trading more — they're about trading better, faster, and with greater control.

Reina's story

Reina sat in her home office, staring at her equity curve. It had taken nearly 18 months, but she had finally built a consistent swing trading strategy. Her win rate hovered near 60%, her risk was tightly managed, and her trading journal was filled with green trades.

But she had a new problem.

Her portfolio was growing, and her strategy was still built for a small account. Managing it manually was becoming overwhelming. She needed a system — one that could scale *without* burning her out.

So, she began building it.

Her first move was segmenting her capital. She created four buckets:

- **Active swing trades**
- **Long-term investments**
- **Stablecoin yield accounts**
- **Small test trades for new strategies**

This alone gave her clarity. No more wondering where to put a promising coin or what risk to use. Each trade now had a *place* and a purpose.

Next, she started using **3Commas**. She connected her Binance and KuCoin accounts via API. Instead of manually entering orders, she built bots that executed her RSI/MACD strategy based on her rules. It took time to configure, but once it ran, it was smooth — no more missed entries or late exits. Alerts triggered actions. Stop-losses were instant.

She didn't go all-in on automation. She started small — letting the bot run a $500 test portfolio. It wasn't perfect, but it worked. Most importantly, it *followed the rules* — every time. No hesitation. No emotion. Just execution.

She also created a custom dashboard in Google Sheets. It tracked equity growth, average R:R, win rate, and monthly drawdown. She reviewed it every Sunday — her new ritual. Just her, her notes, and a quiet cup of tea.

As her confidence grew, she scaled. Not by doubling positions overnight, but slowly — 1% increases after every 10 clean trades. She made a rule: no size increase without discipline first.

Soon, trading became... lighter. Her system worked *with* her. Alerts buzzed when price hit key zones. Her dashboard showed her edge in real-time. Her journal evolved from emotional venting to strategic optimization.

One day, a friend asked her how she was handling the bigger trades. Reina smiled. "It's not me anymore," she said. "It's the system."

And that's when she realized: she hadn't just grown as a trader — she had built a machine. One designed for longevity, powered by discipline, and engineered to scale.

Chapter 11: Creating a Long-Term Career in Crypto Trading

For most people, trading is a temporary obsession — a side hustle, a thrill ride, or a quick-money experiment. But for a small group of individuals, it becomes something more: a **long-term, sustainable career**. Building a trading career requires more than profitable strategies. It demands structure, resilience, ongoing education, and a professional mindset. In this chapter, we'll explore how to transition from trader to trading professional — one with systems, income stability, and longevity in the fast-evolving crypto markets.

The first element of a sustainable trading career is **treating trading like a business**. This means keeping detailed records of every trade, tracking performance metrics, calculating taxes, and reviewing goals monthly or quarterly. Just as a small business evaluates expenses, profits, and customer behavior, a trader must evaluate their **edge, risk exposure, psychological performance, and strategic diversification**.

Next, focus on **multiple revenue streams**. Relying solely on trade profits can create psychological pressure that leads to mistakes. Many full-time traders supplement income by:

- Creating educational content (YouTube, courses, newsletters)
- Offering signals or private coaching (ethically and transparently)
- Building or monetizing trading communities
- Developing and licensing trading bots
- Investing in long-term assets like staking, real estate, or equities

Building these income streams allows you to **trade with less emotional pressure**, because you're not depending on each trade to pay your bills.

Another key principle is **scalability with systems**. A career trader automates tasks wherever possible — from trade journaling, to scanning for setups, to executing strategies via bots or scripts. They develop **playbooks** for different market conditions. For example, they know what to do during low volatility vs. when Bitcoin breaks major support. These playbooks reduce indecision and increase adaptability.

Over time, a trading career should also evolve into **portfolio management**. Rather than thinking in trades, think in allocation. What percentage of your net worth is in active trading? What's in long-term holdings? What's in yield farming or DeFi? What's in stablecoins or emergency funds? Traders who ignore portfolio thinking often become overexposed without realizing it.

Mental resilience becomes more important the longer you trade. You'll encounter unexpected market crashes, brutal drawdowns, regulatory changes, and emotional burnouts. Success requires a long-term mindset — one that emphasizes *process over profit.* Mastery comes not from chasing 10x trades, but from consistent execution through changing conditions.

Also, continue **investing in your education**. Markets evolve. Tools evolve. Strategies that worked in 2021 may fail in 2025. Read books, join mastermind groups, attend virtual events, and stay updated on macroeconomic changes. Lifelong learning is your armor.

Finally, create a **lifestyle that supports trading**. Optimize your sleep, nutrition, exercise, and workspace. Set boundaries around your time and energy. Burnout is real — especially when screens dominate your day. Longevity requires balance.

Trading can be more than a side hustle. It can become a profession — one that offers time freedom, income control, and global mobility. But like any career, it demands **systems,**

discipline, and evolution. Treat it with the respect of a craftsman, and it can serve you for decades.

Jared's long-term crypto career

Jared had been trading for four years. What started as a side gig during the 2020 lockdowns had turned into a full-time pursuit. He no longer had a 9-to-5, but he worked harder than ever. The markets never slept — and neither, it seemed, did he.

At first, the lifestyle was exhilarating. Wake up, trade New York open, take a break, scan charts at night, repeat. But after his first bear market, things changed. His profits dipped. His confidence wavered. And his health? That took a hit too.

That's when Jared decided to stop treating trading like a hobby and start treating it like a career.

He built a proper office — a quiet space with two monitors, a standing desk, and a whiteboard with weekly trade goals. He created a **daily routine**: chart review, pre-market planning, midday walk, and post-trade journaling. He tracked metrics like a CFO: win rate, drawdown, expectancy. His weekends were sacred for review, rest, and strategic planning.

To reduce pressure, he diversified income. He launched a free Substack newsletter that grew into a premium group. He didn't sell signals — just analysis. It was honest, educational, and gave him a side income that covered living expenses. Suddenly, he didn't feel like every trade *had* to work.

He began thinking in **systems**, not signals. He automated trade logging with a Google Sheets API. He used TradingView scripts to send alerts. He wrote protocols for different market types — uptrend, downtrend, sideways — and followed them like a pilot follows a checklist.

His capital grew. He allocated portions to long-term crypto positions, a few stablecoins for yield, and a small DeFi project he believed in. It wasn't all eggs in one basket anymore — it was a diversified *portfolio*.

But the biggest change was internal. Jared no longer got high on wins or crushed by losses. He started meditating. He worked out regularly. He ate better, slept better. Trading wasn't just charts anymore — it was **a lifestyle**, and it had to be sustainable.

One morning, he looked at his journal. Over 800 trades logged. The equity curve was smooth. His bot had just closed a small profit overnight. He sipped coffee, watched the sunrise, and realized — he'd done it.

He hadn't just become a trader. He'd built a **career** — one with systems, balance, and growth. It wasn't about getting rich quick. It was about **staying in the game** long enough to let the numbers compound, let the skills sharpen, and let the freedom bloom.

Chapter 12: The Future of Crypto Trading — Trends, Tech & Global Opportunities

As crypto markets mature, so too does the landscape of professional trading. The edge that once came from simply knowing how to read a candlestick is now shifting toward adaptability, automation, and global awareness. In this final chapter, we look forward — exploring the **future of crypto trading**, the emerging tools, market shifts, and geopolitical trends that forward-thinking traders must prepare for.

1. Rise of AI and Algorithmic Trading

Artificial intelligence is increasingly shaping the way financial markets are traded. AI-driven bots can analyze social sentiment, monitor on-chain activity, and make microsecond trading decisions — far faster than any human. Platforms like **Kronos Research**, **Numerai**, and even open-source AI models are leading this movement.

Retail traders are gaining access to simplified AI tools, such as no-code bot builders, signal copiers, and automated trade management systems. The edge will move from technical setups alone to *who can build smarter, faster systems* that adapt to market behavior in real time.

2. On-Chain Analytics as the New Standard

Future traders will rely heavily on **on-chain data**, which provides transparency and depth that traditional financial markets cannot. Metrics like wallet activity, exchange inflows, smart contract interactions, and governance votes are already becoming integral to pro-level strategies.

New platforms will emerge that offer **real-time on-chain intelligence dashboards**, with alerts for whale movements, token mints, protocol upgrades, and liquidation cascades — all in a single view.

3. Decentralized Trading Infrastructure

The next wave of adoption is headed toward **DEXs (decentralized exchanges)** and **DeFi-native trading**. As users demand more sovereignty, privacy, and non-custodial control, protocols like **dYdX**, **GMX**, **Uniswap v4**, and **Perpetual Protocol** are becoming dominant.

Advanced traders must learn to navigate gas fees, slippage, smart contract risk, and liquidity depth across chains. Tools like **DeBank**, **Zapper**, and **Rabby Wallet** will replace traditional dashboards for those managing DeFi portfolios.

4. Global Regulations & KYC Fragmentation

Crypto trading is becoming increasingly fragmented by **jurisdictional regulations**. Some countries will embrace innovation and provide tax-efficient environments; others will clamp down with capital controls and strict KYC/AML requirements.

Traders must become **geo-strategic**: using VPNs, multi-jurisdictional accounts, international residency, and offshore exchanges to legally optimize access and taxation. The future may require understanding **regulatory arbitrage** as part of your trading toolkit.

5. Tokenization of Everything

From real estate to stocks, commodities, art, and intellectual property, **tokenized assets** will flood the blockchain. Trading won't just be about BTC and ETH — it will involve microshares of buildings, royalties from music NFTs, and even tokenized carbon credits.

Traders who embrace **tokenized asset classes early** will benefit from low competition and high inefficiency — ideal conditions for skilled speculators.

6. New Markets and Time Zones

Crypto is global, and its opportunities are not bound by Wall Street hours. The most active markets may shift toward Asia,

Africa, Latin America, and emerging tech hubs like Dubai or Singapore. Traders fluent in **multiple economic cycles, FX exposure, and local adoption trends** will gain a competitive edge.

Future traders may participate in **real-time AI-powered auctions**, DAO-governed token launches, or time-based liquidity markets — innovations that haven't even reached the mainstream yet.

7. Human Skill Will Still Matter

Despite all the automation, **the best traders will still be those who combine human insight with machine precision**. Pattern recognition, risk tolerance, emotional control, adaptability — these are not easily coded. The winners of tomorrow will blend system thinking with creative strategy.

The future of trading will reward those who invest in **lifelong learning**, rapid adaptation, and interdisciplinary thinking. The tools may evolve — but your edge will always come from how you *use* them.

How Ishan learned to track whale wallets.

Ishan was a veteran trader — not in age, but in experience. He'd lived through DeFi summer, survived the 2022 winter, and rode multiple bull cycles. But lately, something had shifted. It wasn't the market... it was the tools. Everything was changing faster than ever.

His edge used to be chart reading. Now it was **system integration**. He wasn't just a trader anymore — he was building bots, feeding them data from on-chain analytics, and letting them run strategies he used to execute by hand. He still clicked the occasional trade manually — but more often, he monitored dashboards, adjusted parameters, and reviewed performance logs.

Ishan had learned to track whale wallets in real time. He subscribed to on-chain alert services that pinged him when large wallets moved ETH to centralized exchanges. Often, those moves signaled a dump — he'd exit before retail even noticed.

But what really changed his game was **global positioning**. He moved to Portugal for tax advantages, opened an account on a Dubai-based exchange, and learned to read Japanese trading volumes during Asia's peak hours. He wasn't constrained by borders — just bandwidth.

He began experimenting with tokenized assets — buying real estate exposure in Bali, a tokenized farmland share in Argentina, and staking into music NFT royalties. His portfolio looked nothing like it did in 2020.

One night, as he reviewed his setups, a younger trader asked him, “Aren’t you worried bots will replace us?”

Ishan laughed. “They’ll replace the undisciplined. Not the thinkers.”

He leaned back, sipping tea, watching one of his custom bots auto-adjust a trailing stop based on real-time volatility. “The tools will evolve,” he said. “But the game’s still the same — data, risk, and psychology. The only traders who last... are the ones who evolve.”

And with that, he closed his laptop. His system would run overnight. He’d be up at sunrise — not chasing candles, but orchestrating strategy.

He wasn’t just trading anymore.

He was *building the future of trading*.

The Trader You've Become

You've reached the end of Book 8 — not just another chapter, but a milestone in your transformation as a trader.

By now, you've built more than a technical understanding of crypto markets. You've learned how to read patterns, control risk, execute with discipline, manage your emotions, and build scalable systems. But more than any individual skill, you've cultivated a mindset — one of **self-mastery**, **resilience**, and **long-term vision**.

Trading is not a sprint. It's not a lottery ticket. It's a profession. It's a craft. And like all great crafts, it rewards those who commit to the process.

You've seen how to structure entries and exits, automate decision-making, handle fakeouts, and scale your systems. You've explored the psychology of performance and the real-life routines of traders who've made this a sustainable career. And you've looked ahead — at the tools, trends, and global shifts that are redefining what it means to trade in the digital economy.

So what comes next?

It's time to apply what you've learned. Not all at once — but piece by piece. Build your system. Backtest your strategy. Track your trades. Grow your mindset. And remember: every trade is a lesson. Every journal entry is a step forward. Every loss is tuition for a skill that will compound for years.

Let this book serve not just as a guide, but as a **blueprint** for your future in crypto. Come back to it as your capital grows, your strategies evolve, and your confidence expands.

The markets are always moving. But now, so are you — with purpose, preparation, and power.

Welcome to the next level.

www.ingramcontent.com/pod-product-compliance
Lightning Source LLC
LaVergne TN
LVHW022020200926
848481LV00007B/2459
* 9 7 9 8 3 4 9 6 4 4 5 7 3 *